Artisan

Tom Lynch Jr.

RoseDog Books
PITTSBURGH, PENNSYLVANIA 15238

RoseDog Books
585 Alpha Drive
Pittsburgh, PA 15238
Visit our website at *www.rosedogbooks.com*

ISBN: 979-8-88925-289-4
eISBN: 979-8-88925-789-9

Dedicated to life's
eloquently painted brushstrokes
that has given us
our everything forevermore.

Artisan

Hi, I'm Tom Lynch Jr., and I have been writing journals that have led me to live over the rainbow and I have decided to spend my afternoon's time to create an ending to the chronicles of my life's story. I'll start by saying within all that is the story of my life lived, many roles I do play upon the stage, and a few among them are me as a prisoner never free, a wise winged unicorn, as well as the lady goddess divine who knows full well the male admirer is me.

To surmise this perhaps fragmented mirrored view of self would be to say it takes all views to see myself as a whole person today, and with that thought written down in my journal, I took it and my pen and I walked out of the front door to see what awaited me today in this peaceful paradise. It wasn't long before the beauty of all I share with so many here inspired me, and I paused a moment to write. I make all of my plans according to my imagination's wandering wondering, because within is a way to my world of crayon forests with deep puddles of primary color paints, and as I use the branches as brushes, upon the still waiting to be canvas of the rest is created a reflection of a me truly free. I know for an always eternal will my creation's innocence help me have a place of all I dream of, and although at times it may seem complete with its everything artistic, hidden deep in my heart's corners is a replenishing source of new perspectives to paint as my forever home.

With that I continued on to walk over a hill to head towards the playground equipment. Once there, I walked through the park and I stopped to watch some pretty girls pushing each other on swings. After a few moments I sat down on the ground, took my journal and I wrote. To know the wealth of the journey of being over the rainbow is to see, to feel, to understand all of the subtleties and nuances of the artistic expressions offered to you, and when you find yourself there, a chance to embrace its quintessence as your future path is the eventuality of your time well spent. Soon after writing a new poem, the girls and I started talking. Knowing fun as a friend, we decided to take a walk in the woods to admire this land's seasonal change from spring to summer with us being in between both. So beautiful were the white birch trees with some visible darker wood in places helping make this place a truly artistic experience so much so I sat down by a beautiful tree to write.

I personally believe there is no such thing as justifiable anger, and my reasoning behind this is life will always offer us a higher path in all situations, understanding of course it's always up to us to use our freewill to walk that higher path. As our time there met the moment I was to walk in a new direction, we all hugged and said to each other, "see you soon," and upon a new path I did go to find Queen Cinnamony Stuff writing as well.

She did ask me, "Does all that is night's nocturnal beauty fade with the morning's brighter expressions, or perhaps is day simply the rest of the poem that is a twenty-four's time?" and I did answer her by saying, "When springtime comes from winter's frost to become new renewal which wends its way towards smooth feeling summer experiences and that becomes autumn's array of colors, scents and sounds all around. And as a family of family of friends we go to the local farm and partake in the experience of helping with the harvest of fresh peaches, as well as all of the offerings to pick that eventually become a knowing of making and enjoying holiday dinners with others within each other's homes as the fresh fallen snow is becoming another winter's wonderland. We experience an all-encompassing of everything that truly shows us life's continuity."

With my goddess going on her way to more inspiring thoughts to be found, I went on to write, as we are on our way within our round windowed silver ship to a many color crystal planet. We spend given time talking about the soon to be future of us having underwater adventures while swimming in its prism rainbow oceans, rivers and lakes. As always lying waiting are fields of fresh green grass so soft with pretty flowers all around, well known to enrich the scent of all as we play, and when a secret door within a wall we find along our way sublime.

Off we will be into the haunted hills of Halloween to run under darkened starry skies being Boonicorns, and to properly set the mood the shared ghostly galloping off to a destination unknown is to our song a haunting we will go, sung with choir-like singing which is all that we knew before improved.

When we are sailing back to where we came, it will be with the bestowence of knowledge. Imagination as all around is the ultimate fun and with that I walked to an area with waterfalls the colors of sugary sweet lemon, raspberry, strawberry and pure blue falling from above. All around where the four rivers continued to flow was a pool of water from each, and standing there admiring the pleasant scene were four girls with the names Aurora, Abigail, Angie and Anabelle, all wearing string bikinis of reflective colors the same. Each in turn gave me a warm embrace, and the love they so freely gave to me was enough to inspire all of my dreams to come true. I gave an equally as heartfelt response to each, and moments after the last hug was given I did say, "It's nice to see you Angie from the land of Hearts and Love." She then responded to me with a kiss and I did say to her, "I have recently written a new poem for you." So with a quick reach into my bag I retrieved my journal and said to her, "My cinnamony dreamy, she with her soft sweetness as rose petal ice cream, always has me feeling her realm, known as her warmth of love's perfect tranquility, and as I live within all she is, it is with the knowledge when at each day's end I sleep a deep slumber. It will be with the blessings of my beloved angelic Angie."

With that added to our lives together within this warm summer's day we spent together, we decided to go to the waterfall of pure blue. Once within nature's natural pool, so cool was the water cascading upon us from above, and at some point from then to my now, with pen in hand, I used the moment's memory to write a new poem. So I got my journal and wrote.

With my blue blankie as a cape, I flew to a beautiful land I had heard about that was beyond the moon, and when to my destination new I did get, the first thing I noticed was here all of the houses had a candy-like look. As I walked around and admired it all, I was enchanted with the presence of a Princess Mage who said her name was Kari, and she did say to me as a hello, welcome to the age of ultra-magic and as she spoke, all around majestic music I did hear. Soon she did say, "Tell me a bit about yourself, newcomer to my land," and so I replied, "My name is Tommy Lynch Jr.," and I then told her many things about me, including my favorite color is blue, my favorite monsters are Munsters and they live at 1313 Mockingbird Lane and perhaps it's not so strange for I'm the fruity minded sort of person you see, because my mind is from an over the rainbow me and one day I plan to be marooned in a cartoon floating while boating on a crayon colored sea, thinking such thoughts as, I look at the sky with its complete cloud cover today and instead of being gloomy

I will simply remember above the pillowy blanket is all clear sky and sunshine.

With this from me to her, she did write a note and said it was mine to keep and it read, "I'm keeping an I on U, so I'll give you this unique letter that will just need a heart to say I love you and perhaps, I'll use my own since it now belongs to the kid with eyes of blue" and with a small travel I made my way behind my house to the tree with the tire swing, I noticed a door in the tree that had not been there before. Being the adventuresome me I am, I opened it and walked through to find myself wandering within a fog filled moonlit night to find in the distance an old mansion that seemed to me to be a grave and a collection of cracked tombstones created a walkway to the decrepit porch worn out and ruined by ages of neglect.

With my walk upon them, I traversed to a door that creaked when opened. I did see dusty cobwebbed barriers in every doorway, and I soon knew ages of time have passed here with the same measured moments as the outer world, but here only stillness resides. Within a look all around could be seen. The last life this place knew and the placement of objects were unchanged, preserved for those who venture here to see, all while feeling the oppressive unmoving air all around seeming to almost have a heaviness to it. As I moved through the thick, suddenly there was to hear across the room spooky sounding chimes from Victorian orchestrina tines which seemed to almost have us rejoin the flow of time that moments ago seemed a timeless prison. With this thought, I noticed what seemed to be a well-worn dust coated diary on a small table near me and it was open to the last entry which read as follows.

The storybook of my dream's nature that brought a magical essence across the once flowering field of my life, now with equal an abundance only brings a seemingly wrought with lost lonely shadows barren wasteland, and as I try to reclaim all that was amidst fragments of things heard here from the disjointed despair of the always drifting apparitions, I choose to take this timelessness and reclaim it all back to a place that feels more like how I long to see myself once again, but I know both views say so much about me. So with this knowing, I sit on a stump of what was the once tall tree of life, and as an old man I remember being a little boy playing with a paper bird with such joyful freedom. As I do, it seems the nature of fate screams to me I'm destined to feel as an anchorless boat adrift amidst all that does separate. I continue all the while through the broken clocks long days trying to regain my former sense of self. Such an experience is much like remembering a home I never had; however, I know the day will come when I can recreate all around me and then I shall be in a place where all amidst the houses will have a fantasy feel, like a nice summer day from a dream and always from then will this strange be changed and rearranged to the vibe of time passing enriching all with a vintage feel and then my life will collectively be comforted knowing so cool is everything's now poetically bejeweled old school.

With this heavily on my mind, I made my way through the kitchen to the back of the house. With a few steps out a back door, I could see out on the back forty a haunted horseman wearing a tattered threadbare frock coat seemingly caught within a time of his own, carrying out actions of perhaps to him a better vanished part of his life. Above the sky had a look of emerald fire. All the while watching him I did wonder if he ever ventured inside his home to act out his own semblance of his life long ago known, and with this thought I went back the way I came as slowly as I could as not to disturb the way I found things. So preserved can be whatever he was clinging onto as his only memory left to him, out of respect I guess of the mutual feelings he and I shared, feelings of loneliness, longing and a need to escape eternal abandonment. At least this is how things seem to me, and so on the front porch I chronicled in this journal, *Artisan*, what I had seen and known almost as if I was knowing what it must have been like when all was new, and perhaps this experience happened through feelings left behind by those that had once brought life to this place.

With a short walk down the aged collection of cracked tombstones, I walked back through the fog-filled night to the door in the tree with the old tire swing seen on this side as being equal to everything else here. Once on the opposite side, everything was again to me as a bright sun-filled summer day with the same tire swing offering me the purity of a fun's time, and when I looked back at the tree, the door was no more and looking now at a tree more normal. I think perhaps with time's gentler understandings I know I shall dream one night of what my time spent there meant, for a dream is an answer to a question we have yet to ask.

Onward I went to admire the pure blue sky. So moved by the moment's beauty, I sat down and penned the following poem.

As daylight is dawning with us asleep on soft pink silk sheets, we awaken to a new day, and as we see each other within this morning new, I do get up and go to the window to see the new morning's dew. I then turn to her to see mocha Maria sensuously gesturing me over to thee. As I am soon with her on our bed, I take the moment to say, "The reason you I did wed was to live our life together in such a way as to always say, all she is, a way of saying the softest of love's gentleness is a girl and with the admiring of my she." I always must let her know this is understood unto my soul and this will be done with everything from the grandest expressions to something as simple as a warm embrace, for I know to see a female is to be honorable and respectful with all of my ways, so know my beloved all that is in my mind exists around and through eternal time, because my love's heart is intertwined with all that is infinite creation divine. Good morning, my goddess of angelic design.

It was at this time within the adventure of my life I asked myself what I'm living is all about, and I did say as a response, "Within the dark depths of all that is unknown to us all lies a hidden vault of meaningful things unsaid, and within this treasure trove of purity's essence as yet to unfold as a rose and have its life be part of the artistic fabric of our many friendship's together lived is a small unheard voice saying, 'please release me, let me go.' So all may know my lessons that are here to enrich all souls lucid and for us to make paths that illuminate the way there, know the secret to have the door's lock be opposite of not get in and have all within no longer seeming a cryptic secret is. Everyone's arms open to each other with a mutual expressed 'I love you,' and when that moment is to us past, present or future to be, with this simple knowledge will the poetry be flowing free, poetry that says, once we step inside life's candy shop all will have the thought, each treat is sweet, much like all that lingers after each kiss upon your lady's feet.

It was at this time I decided to visit the land known as a rainbow's rose where there was goddess of love, sensually sexy cinnamon Selena bestowing guidance as a gift with her nurturing allure through devotion's essence. As I started on the path of twinkling starlight that led to her homeland, a feeling of warm and welcoming breathlessness from my heart always true brought crystalline tears of gentleness from blue eyes that now know only passionate expressions of imagination's innocence, laughter's happiness and sensitivity's sincerity, so with a pleasant walk feeling freedom's contentment I admired this land's treasures of many artistic journeys to know, all from the creative expressions of those who live here in this treasured land.

Once to my destination I did get, I went inside her ice cream castle and soon with my heart so pure I was in the presence of her elegant transcendence that is her purity's grace. I did feel such passionate acceptance in the form of nourishing peacefulness from Goddess Selena for all that I am as a person living within love's eternal hope. Upon her throne of love and trust, she was beauty within honesty looking like a dream's wish with her classic cat eye framed glasses, a perfect complement to her pink paisley groovy go-go dress and mod boots with all she is having the scent and sight of a rose petal's softness, truly an expression of artful sexiness. This girl, who found strength within her beauty that I found myself standing before, filled me with anticipation of inspiration and she did say to me, "A snuggle's warmth awaits you because I can clearly see upon hope's essence do you await my feminine approval, and since you have sought me with a true heart that's perhaps a bit more innocent than those that share the world you are from, so let your heart's concerns know only caring's dreaming, for you are now within the kingdom of Goddess Selena."

She beckoned me closer as she got up from her throne with me walking towards her and I was soon feeling reassurance's confidence as she shared with me a warm embrace and soft affectionate tenderness and in that moment I felt Heaven's love within her kisses. The feeling told me of a brighter future's dream telling me that love triumphs over all. Soon after she returned to her grand place within her palace.

I did say, "I have a poem as an expression of my heart's wishes for you," and she listened intently as I said, "Loving expressions from the journey of life I have brought that are from my visions of dreaming with each dream being a heart's reflection, so let me take you there so you may have a true path home to know friendship as a treasure. The first offering will be to let you hear as love's prayer the words spoken. I do adore lying next to you always and forever in love with our auras glistening as sparkles from a color palette's glitter paint under the light of cupid's playfulness, knowing the quiet contentment I feel hearing you say to me 'I love you' to and as a response I let you know to hold you in my arms and kiss you so softly amidst whispered promises of hope, unity's sincerity and angelic visions of us walking within the moonlight's glimmer knowing a rose's treasures as love all around is to be loved for who I am within. As I gaze upon you, do know all I see within the silk lace you wear is the essence of a woman who knows I want to be intimately loved by her forever." With her encouragement's friendship, she tells me I am a dream's essence of such uniqueness, so with my wishes of caring and adoration I do tell her, "The mystique of your passions are seen all around you as reflections of jewels, and when we part ways seeming ever longer are the days until I see you again, but once more am I put at ease with thoughts of your loving beauty, which is to me, a pure love hereafter. I'm feeling only purity of thought until we meet again, for such is the path of a dreamer."

I did continue with saying "a second poem for you," and Selena responded with a wink. I did recite to her yet another offering, with a simple, "Perhaps it was a community of people sharing memories of our wedding that reminded me of our first hello that ended with a simple until next time and in between I said to you, I'm a creating artisan and all I do brings such comfort to many, with all of my offerings being reflections of self, which all started as a faint glimmering within, yearning for creativity's honest understanding bringing with it inspiration's enlightenment saying hope's promises are as peacefulness to me and with great fondness towards me you said. Expressions of your artistry are as you with both being the art of love's light."

I did say, "When I hold you close and whisper a soft spoken beauty is yours, I know with love one giveth life for the journey, so know I've saved some kisses for you, although I know a heart never forgets true love and when the day comes ours is no longer a love affair from afar. The sweet scent of you will be felt so gentle unto all of my life's dreams and forever remember fulfilled is creative enlightenment embracing sensitivity. So until we meet again, remember among life's most blessed expressions to me are softness, playfulness, honesty's caring comfort and kissable you so soft, to which you responded, "Compassion's beauty always encourages wisdom's life and always offers all to feel love's bravery." Looking back, perhaps it was because of these words shared that we returned to each other and have become what has been our long life together."

Writing now after my time with her was brought to this moment's fruition, I can honestly say if you have yet to meet her, know she's a lady. Of this be assured, and with poetry's essence within me flowing free, I wrote more to be able to say. Inside my mind I find honesty reflected as thoughts pure, thoughts such as my life is a groovy movie and among today's more memorable scenes were starting the morning with my baker's dozen of thirteen, leaving one for me, and I enjoyed it as I drank my toffee-flavored coffee. The afternoon then held for me time at the ice cream parlor watching colorful shades of happy delightfully dancing all around, as well as seeing a ballet at the chalet, and of course afterwards I drove my car to a magical star to express myself with my sapphire guitar.

On my return trip, I stopped by a friend's house to see pure blue sky through the tree's branches, and as I walked with her through the hundred acre wood, the sights and sounds of the forest were all enhanced by the flowing water of a creek. It was all such a delicate musical feel, and after our walk I did say to her, "Just follow dreaming me to a field of glow in the dark flowers of every color that can be," and when a few more she's we do see, I will weave the petals and stems into a boat with a mast and we'll sail across a fantasy sea to the land of eternal sensuality and reader remember. You know this all to be true for you like me are wise enough to see within our imagination's limitless nature are we forever free.

Now with me back at my colorful home over the rainbow, I sat on my front porch to write another poem that reads, "I'm a traveler who feels like an old anvil with its original hammer, both well worn, trying to get back to where he started. As I wend my way forward with passionate perseverance, the key for a loving going forward is honesty pure, true and free. As collected experiences make a whole, known as my life's beliefs finding magical paths of stardust are a must and find one I will by simply continuing to see with my inner inspiration that will one day have sparkles beneath my footsteps that take me to where I need to be and that being in Oakdale, Minnesota walking to a small house on 7th Street, where my young and old self will exchange wisdom from experience. Then the causality of cause and effect along with the intertwining thought original imagery from my childhood imagination has helped to create my creative today, will have me knowing a perfect paradise of a destination as an older version of a younger me who can go back and forth seamlessly."

That will then be the time I know I shall meet my true love and Hispanic her with cinnamon curves so smooth wearing bright cherry red lipstick perhaps enriching music by a mystical looking candle's greenish glow, and she shall say to me, living in a happy haunted mansion is what I do and my ghostly guests are more than a few, because they all know as you." Every day is a Halloween's celebration, because it creates the other three sixty four's rescue, then with her hand in mine will we take a side trip through time by creating a temporal shift and go to a world where happy memories of her and I are making towers of flowers with Goddess Cherry Blossom. So whether I be here, there or anywhere, once worn out old me will be found saying to my lady "tickle me here tickle me there, because I'm your big cuddly teddy bear," so with my afternoon's time almost spent writing one last journal, a visitor I did get and I have preserved what I said here in this journal:

"Queen Cinnamony Stuff has given me a chance to speak to everyone over the rainbow so here it goes. To all of those I've met since arriving here and to those I have yet to meet, a wise man once said, there's not a word yet for old friends who've just met. With that said, I'll continue by asking you all, have you ever been on a long hard journey you thought you wouldn't make it through? I know I have, and amidst all the trials, tribulations with the hardships as the only thing to be seen as well as felt, almost bringing you to a point you became convinced you were building a bridge across forever and amidst what seemed like still stood all time. At the end with your goals accomplished, it was with the realization that the entire time there wasn't a moment you spent alone, and perhaps that's because love is the knowledge true friends are always with you although sometimes seemingly unseen but still forever there. I know each of you has been there for me in your own way, so let us now move on with what we've learned together to a happy forevermore."

I continued to address the crowd by saying, "To conclude, I will recite a poem I wrote recently: I'm living all of my dreams, because I followed the words in my head when they said, I live in a tree you see to get a better view of all that is you and me and a treasure map for you is now your intellectual intellect, derivative of your eternal younger than old life. This path has led to a self-created empire from my imaginary imagery from my kid to now life and all that is truly mine will stand for all time to be a home for innocence divine and always within this love's land where the sun and moon shine like sparkling magical translucent sand will you see my immortal me with my band getting groovy with all of the colorful gummy bears delightfully dancing so grand."

With thunderous applause from the crowd, I simply stood and knew my life would forever be fantasy stuff all around, and so, journal reader, you may be wondering what the poetry I've been writing along with the tales of my continued travels to be added to my tomes has to do with the title of this newest offering of mine. It's all been to help create a better, more imaginative version of life, so all she is has a better day to dance within. As for me, I'm quite content with this being my last journal I will write. Why, you may ask, is this my last? Because it's only with the final brushstroke the painting can be complete, for only then can we step back and admire with others what the artist is saying, and perhaps this is a way of understanding all that is eternal through a finite expression. With a fundamental point being the artist is an admirer as well, and it's now time for me to start to embrace the wisdom I have discovered and expressed in my collection of books that has led me over the rainbow. So until the day comes we are all here together, always stay poetically colorful with all of your life's expressions, and perhaps the moral of the story is that fantasy can truly mirror reality and reality can mirror fantasy, all while we wend our way forward toward a future for humanity, knowing the path to living our dreams will always be to infinity and beyond, with us living as love's artisans.

www.ingramcontent.com/pod-product-compliance
Lightning Source LLC
Chambersburg PA
CBHW071229140726
47996CB00004B/1532